THE KETOGENIC MEXICAN COOKBOOK

60 Low Carb and Delicious Mexican Dishes

TABLE OF CONTENTS

INTRODUCTION

This book contains a variety of recipes to satisfy your cravings for Mexican dishes without breaking your ketogenic diet.

Ketogenic is a popular diet that many people have already benefitted from. It is more than a diet because it is a lifestyle. Once you get into the habit, you will start reaping most of its health benefits, including weight loss. You can tweak the meals served depending on your preference.

This book offers 60 Mexican recipes for appetizer, breakfast, main dish, soup, dessert, and beverages. The recipes are easy to follow and contain nutritional information to make it easier for you to monitor your carb and nutrient intake.

Thanks for purchasing this book, I hope you enjoy it!

CHAPTER 1

BRIEF INTRODUCTION ABOUT THE KETOGENIC DIET

The ketogenic diet requires low-carb, moderate protein, and high fat intake. This popular diet program offers tons of health benefits, including weight loss. Your body will find it easier to get into the state of ketosis when it gets a minimal amount of carbohydrates. As a result, your system will burn your stored fat for energy, and convert them into ketones in the liver. The body utilizes the ketones to supply energy to the brain when you are on this kind of diet.

Your body naturally creates ketones when it is in the state of ketosis. As the ketones surge in your system, your insulin and blood sugar levels get lower. The state of ketosis is what makes the diet unique. Your body does not make ketones when you are on a regular diet. It decides on how much fat it will burn.

Your system will automatically look for an alternative energy source when you are taking a limited amount of carbs. It will enter the state of ketosis to keep up with your body's supply of energy, and in the process, it will produce ketones. The human body also enters the state of ketosis after being engaged in a tiring physical activity for a long time.

Ketosis is what makes the ketogenic diet effective as a weight loss program. It suppresses your appetite and helps in building up muscles. As long as you are healthy, you don't have diabetes, and are not pregnant, you can reach this metabolic state three days after you start consuming less than 50 grams of carb per day.

The Benefits of the Diet

Aside from weight loss, the diet also offers the following health benefits:

1. It boosts your HDL levels and decreases your LDL levels. LDL is the bad cholesterol. A significant drop in your LDL levels comes as a result of too much consumption of saturated fat and limited intake of sugar. This will increase the levels of your good cholesterol or HDL. To maintain good health of the heart, maintain a ratio of more than 39 mg of HDL over your LDL.

2. The diet is effective in maintaining good levels of blood pressure. Make sure that you consult with a doctor first if you are taking medications for blood pressure and the heart before starting with the diet.

3. The diet gives you more energy even though you are eating less food. It also alleviates joint and muscle pains, and helps in treating health conditions, such as chronic fatigue.

4. The diet improves the quality of your sleep.

5. It gives you a clearer mind and a better mood. The diet is both neurotherapeutic and neuroprotective. It boosts the health of your brain. It is also effective in reducing the swelling of the brain caused by migraines and certain traumatic injuries.

There have been studies that prove that the diet could help improve the symptoms of the following conditions:

- Heart ailments
- Alzheimer's disease
- Polycystic ovary syndrome
- Parkinson's disease
- Cancer
- Brain injuries
- Acne

The Ketogenic Diet for Mexican Food Lovers

You can adapt the diet no matter what kinds of dishes you're craving for. You will not run out of Mexican meals as long as you follow these rules:

1. Cook food on a skillet or grill them. Avoid or limit your consumption of tortillas, rice, and beans.
2. You can always add flavor to make your dishes Mexican. Top favorites include shredded cheese, chimichurri, sour cream, guacamole, and salsa fresca.
3. It is better to make your own seasoning and flavors to avoid products with carb-dense flour and high sugar content.
4. Replace chips with chicharrones or pork rinds. You can also start snacking on low-carb veggies, such as romaine lettuce spears, jicama, radishes, cucumbers, and celery.

Watch out for the following carb-dense items when you are on a ketogenic diet. You can replace them with healthier options fit for the diet:

- Most desserts and special cocktails
- Aquas Frescas
- Horchatas
- Fruit juice
- Fruit-based salsa

- Yucca
- Bananas
- Plantains
- Sweet dressings
- Fruity drinks
- Picadillos
- Enchiladas
- Quesadillas
- Empanadas
- Tamales

CHAPTER 2

APPETIZER RECIPES

SLOW-COOKER TACO PEPPER WITH STUFFING

Yield: 6 servings
Preparation time: 10 minutes
Cooking Time: 4 or 8 hours

INGREDIENTS:

- 1 1/2 tablespoons olive oil
- 1 teaspoon chili powder
- 1 teaspoon garlic powder
- 1 cup Monterey jack cheese (shredded)
- 1 cup water
- 500 grams turkey (minced)
- 1 cup cauliflower rice
- 6 small red bell peppers (remove the stems and seeds)

DIRECTIONS:

1. Put the meat in a bowl. Add the spices and rub all over. Add olive oil and cauliflower. Mix thoroughly. Gently mix the shredded cheese.
2. Arrange the hollow shells of bell peppers on a plate. Stuff each piece with the mixture.
3. Place the stuffed peppers in a crockpot. Put a cup of water in the pot's bottom part. You can cook it for 4 hours on a high-temperature setting or 8 hours on a low setting.

4. Open the pot 10 minutes before the cooking is done. Sprinkle cheese on top of each piece and continue cooking.

Nutri info per serving (1 piece): 250 calories, 4.02g net carbs, 15.8g fat, 22.19g protein

VERY VEGETARIAN TACO

Yield: 1 serving
Preparation time: 10 minutes
Cooking Time: 15 minutes

INGREDIENTS:

For the avocado boats

- 1 tablespoon cheddar cheese (shredded)
- 1 tablespoon sour cream
- 1/2 avocado (medium)
- 1/2 cup taco filling

For the filling

- 1 teaspoon salt
- 2 tablespoons cheddar cheese (shredded)
- 4 tablespoon avocado oil (divided)
- 2 teaspoons adobo sauce
- 2 teaspoons smoked paprika
- 1 teaspoon onion powder
- 1 teaspoon garlic powder
- 1 teaspoon cumin
- 1 tablespoon hemp seeds (hulled)
- 1 cup raw walnuts
- 7 ounces cauliflower (cut into florets)

DIRECTIONS:

1. Prepare the filling. Put the hemp seeds, raw walnuts, cauliflower florets, and seasonings in a food processor. Pulse until crumbled.
2. Put half of the oil in a pan over medium flame. Once heated, put half of the processed mixture. Cook until the cauliflower is cooked and the nuts are toasted. Fold in half of the adobo sauce. Cook until both sides are browned. Transfer to a bowl and add salt and cheese.

3. Cook the remaining filling.
4. Scoop out the avocado meat to make the boat. Slice meat and reserve to be used as topping.
5. Put half a cup of the filling in the avocado boat. Top with cheese, sour cream, and avocado slices.

Nutri info per serving: 392.17 calories, 6.3g net carbs, 46.49g fat, 13.23g protein

FRIED MEXICAN CHEESE

Yield: 5 servings
Preparation time: 2 minutes
Cooking Time: 5 minutes

INGREDIENTS:

- 1/2 tablespoon olive oil
- 1 tablespoon coconut oil
- 1 pound queso fresco (cut into cubes)

DIRECTIONS:

1. Put olive oil and coconut oil in a pan over high flame. Add cheese once heated. Cook until both sides are browned. Transfer to a plate lined with paper towels.

Nutri info per serving: 307 calories, 2.7g net carbs, 25.63g fat, 16.39g protein

ROASTED GARLIC GUACAMOLE WITH BACON SALAD

Yield: 3 servings
Preparation time: 15 minutes
Cooking time: 10 minutes

INGREDIENTS:

- 1/3 cup cilantro (chopped)
- 1 tablespoon roasted garlic
- 1/4 onion (thinly sliced)
- 1/3 medium red bell pepper (sliced)
- Salt and pepper to taste
- 1/2 lime (juiced)
- 4 bacon slices (cut into small cubes)
- 2 Hass avocados (medium)

DIRECTIONS:

1. Heat pan over medium flame. Cook the bacon slices until crisp. Set aside.
2. Slice the avocados and scoop out meat into a bowl. Crush the roasted garlic and add to the bowl. Add the bell pepper, cilantro, onion, and cooked bacon with the grease. Gently toss until combined.
3. Season with salt and pepper, and add lime juice before serving.

Nutri info per serving: 225 calories, 4.55g net carbs, 18.74g fat, 6.12g protein

YUMMY GUACAMOLE

Yield: 2 cups
Preparation time: 15 minutes

INGREDIENTS:

- 1 tablespoon fresh lime juice
- 2 tablespoons salsa
- 1 medium jalapeño (diced)
- 1/3 medium red onion (thinly sliced)
- 1/2 bunch (0.5-ounce) fresh cilantro (coarsely chopped)
- Salt and pepper to taste
- 2 whole Hass avocados

DIRECTIONS:

1. Scoop out avocado meat, put in a bowl, and mash using a fork. Add the diced jalapeño, sliced onion, salsa, and lime juice. Mix well. Stir in the chopped cilantro.

Nutri info per serving (1 tablespoon): 16.56 calories, 0.48g net carbs, 1.41g fat, 0.23g protein

KETO-FRIENDLY MEXICAN CAULI RICE

Yield: 4 servings
Preparation time: 15 minutes
Cooking Time: 15 minutes

INGREDIENTS:

- 450 grams cauliflower rice
- 1 teaspoon cumin
- 1 tablespoon chili powder
- 1 garlic clove (minced)
- 1/2 medium white onion (diced)
- 2 tablespoons extra virgin olive oil
- Sea salt to taste
- 1 14.5-ounce can diced tomatoes (no salt added)

Optional toppings

- Extra virgin olive oil
- Jalapeno slices
- Sour cream
- Avocado slices
- Minced cilantro
- Lime wedges

DIRECTIONS:

1. Put oil in a skillet over medium flame. Once heated, add onion and stir for a couple of minutes or until soft. Add the spices and cook until fragrant. Stir in cauliflower rice. Cook for 7 minutes or until the edges are crisp. Add the diced tomatoes and gently mix until combined. Cook for 5 minutes.

2. Season with salt and add your preferred toppings before serving.

You can place the leftovers in a container and store in the fridge to last up to 4 days.

Nutri info per serving (1 cup): 120 calories, 7g net carbs, 7.7g fat, 3.6g protein

JALAPEÑO POPPERS WITH CHICKEN STUFFING

Yield: 15 poppers
Preparation time: 15 minutes
Cooking Time: 20 minutes

INGREDIENTS:

- 1 teaspoon Cajun seasoning
- 1/2 teaspoon kosher salt (adjust according to taste)
- 1/2 teaspoon garlic powder
- 1/3 cup salsa verde

- 2 cups cooked chicken (shredded and chopped)
- 8 ounces cream cheese (room temperature)
- 1 cup sharp cheddar cheese (grated)
- 15 jalapeño pepper (large)

For the breading

- 1/2 teaspoon Cajun seasoning

- 1 cup pork rinds (pulverized)

DIRECTIONS:

1. Slice a bit of the top part of each pepper and scoop out the meat. Arrange them on a heatproof plate and microwave for 2 minutes.
2. Prepare the stuffing. Put cream cheese and cheddar cheese in a bowl. Mix until creamy. Add Cajun seasoning, garlic powder, salsa verde, and cooked chicken. Mix until blended.
3. Combine the ingredients for the breading in a small bowl.
4. Add stuffing mixture to each jalapeño pepper. Dip the filling part to the breading mixture. Arrange on a tray and bake for 20 minutes at 400 F.

5. Leave for 5 minutes before serving.

Nutri info per serving (1 popper): 111 calories, 1g net carbs, 9g fat, 6g protein

SPICY MEXICAN SLAW

Yield: 6 servings
Preparation time: 15 minutes

INGREDIENTS:

For the salad

- 1/2 cup cilantro (rinsed and chopped)
- 2 green onions (thinly sliced)
- 2 cups red cabbage (thinly sliced)
- 4 cups green cabbage (thinly sliced)

For the dressing

- 1/2 teaspoon hot sauce (adjust according to taste)
- 3 tablespoon fresh lime juice
- 4 tablespoon mayonnaise
- Sea salt to taste

DIRECTIONS:

1. Prepare the dressing. Put mayonnaise in a cup. Gradually add hot sauce and lime juice as you whisk. Adjust amount according to taste.
2. Put cilantro, green onions, and cabbage in a salad bowl. Add the dressing and toss until combined. Season with salt.

Nutri info per serving (1 cup): 104 calories, 10g net carbs, 7g fat, 2g protein

LOW CARB CAULIFLOWER SKEWERS

Yield: 4 servings
Preparation time: 15 minutes

INGREDIENTS:

- 2 tablespoon fresh cilantro (chopped)
- 4 lime wedges
- 1/3 cup Cotija cheese (finely crumbled)
- 1 teaspoon kosher salt (adjust according to taste)
- 1 tablespoon ground chipotle pepper powder
- 1 tablespoon granulated Erythritol sweetener
- 1/4 cup mayonnaise
- 2 cups cauliflower florets (cooked)

DIRECTIONS:

1. Put the cooked cauliflower florets on 4 skewers.
2. Put the sweetener and mayonnaise in a small bowl. Mix until combined. Brush all sides of the cauliflower florets with the mixture.
3. Coat the florets with crumbled cheese and sprinkle with salt and chipotle powder. Squeeze juice of 1 lime in each skewer.
4. Place the cauliflower skewers on a plate, add cilantro on top, and serve while warm.

Nutri info per serving (1/2 cup or 1 skewer): 139 calories, 2g net carbs, 15g fat, 5g protein

LOW CARB TAQUITOS

Yield: 1 dozen
Preparation time: 15 minutes
Cooking Time: 30 minutes

INGREDIENTS:

- 2/3 cup red enchilada sauce
- 2 cups chicken (shredded)
- 1 teaspoon chili powder
- 1 teaspoon ground cumin
- 4 garlic cloves (minced)
- 1/2 onion (minced)
- 2 tablespoons extra-virgin olive oil
- 2 cups Monterey jack cheese (shredded)
- 2 cups cheddar cheese (shredded)
- Kosher salt to taste
- 4 tablespoons cilantro (chopped, add more for garnishing)

DIRECTIONS:

1. Prepare the dipping sauce. Put oil in a pan over medium flame. Add minced onion once heated, and cook for 3 minutes. Add spices and garlic. Cook for a couple of minutes. Stir in enchilada sauce, reduce heat to low, and leave to simmer for 3 minutes. Remove from heat. Season with salt, and add the chopped cilantro.
2. Prepare the taquito shells. Put all the shredded cheese in a bowl and mix well. Divide into 12.
3. Line two baking sheets with parchment paper. Make 12 cheese piles with 3.5-inch height. Bake in a preheated oven at 375 F for 10 minutes. Leave to cool for 4 minutes before peeling off each shell.

4. Put a small pile of shredded meat to each shell. Roll them tightly. Arrange the taquitos on a plate. Drizzle with sauce and top with chopped cilantro.

Nutri info per serving (1 piece): 230 calories, 2g net carbs, 18g fat, 17g protein

CHAPTER 3

BREAKFAST RECIPES

TACO-FLAVORED EGG MUFFINS

Yield: 6 servings
Preparation time: 15 minutes
Cooking Time: 25 minutes

INGREDIENTS:

- 1/2 cup salsa
- 1/2 cup sour cream
- 10 black olives (sliced)
- 3 ounces mixed bell peppers (chopped)
- 1 cup shredded sharp cheddar cheese
- 12 large eggs
- 2 ounces onion (minced)
- 3 tablespoons Taco Seasoning
- 8 ounces ground beef

DIRECTIONS:

1. Cook onions and meat in a skillet over medium-high flame until browned. Remove excess grease from the skillet before adding taco seasoning and 1/3 cup water. Turn heat to low and leave to simmer for 4 minutes.
2. Whisk eggs in a bowl. Gradually add olives, bell peppers, and cheese. Add the cooked meat and onion. Mix well.

3. Transfer mixture to 12 lightly greased muffin tins. Bake
    in a preheated oven at 350 F for 25 minutes.
4. Top with salsa and sour cream before serving.

Nutri info per serving (2 muffins): 330 calories, 6g net carbs, 17g fat, 21g protein

MEXICAN CHORIZO CHEESE OMELET

Yield: 8 slices
Preparation time: 15 minutes
Cooking Time: 40 minutes

INGREDIENTS:

- 12 large eggs
- 1/4 teaspoon black pepper
- 1/4 teaspoon sea salt
- 1 cup grated cheddar cheese
- 2 garlic cloves (minced)
- 1 yellow onion (chopped)

- 2 tablespoons ghee
- 200 grams dark leaf kale (discard the stems, rinse, and tear into smaller pieces)
- 225 grams Mexican chorizo sausage (crumbled)

Optional toppings

- Sriracha sauce
- Guacamole
- Sour cream

- Diced peppers, cherry tomatoes, or avocado

DIRECTIONS:

1. Put ghee in a casserole dish over medium-high flame. Once heated, add onion, and cook for 5 minutes. Stir in garlic and continue cooking for 1 minute. Add the crumbled sausage. Cook for 5 minutes while stirring often. Add kale. Reduce heat to medium-low and cover the dish. Cook for 15 minutes.
2. Whisk eggs in a bowl. Season with salt and pepper. Pour the mixture over the chorizo in the casserole dish. Stir in

grated cheddar cheese. Sprinkle the remaining cheese on top. Bake in a preheated oven at 350 F for 15 minutes.

3. Slice and top with your preferred toppings before serving.

Nutri info per serving (1 slice): 285 calories, 3g net carbs, 21.5g fat, 18.2g protein

JALAPEÑO POPPER FRITTATA

Yield: 4 servings
Preparation time: 15 minutes
Cooking Time: 35 minutes

INGREDIENTS:

For the egg custard

- 1/8 teaspoon ground black pepper
- 1/4 teaspoon Kosher salt
- 2 tablespoons heavy whipping cream
- 1/3 cup unsweetened almond milk
- 6 eggs

For the filling

- 1/4 cup sharp cheddar cheese (shredded)
- 2 tablespoons salsa verde
- 2 tablespoons jalapeño peppers (chopped)
- 6 ounces cream cheese (room temperature)

For toppings

- 1/2 cup sharp cheddar cheese (shredded)
- 6 bacon slices (fried and chopped)
- 1 tablespoon jalapeños (sliced)

DIRECTIONS:

1. In a bowl, mix 1/4 cup shredded cheddar cheese, salsa verde, jalapeños, and cream cheese. Heat in the microwave for a minute. Mix until smooth.

2. Whisk eggs in another bowl. Add salt, pepper, heavy cream, and almond milk. Whisk until smooth.
3. Transfer the cheese mixture to a greased casserole dish and spread out evenly. Pour the egg mixture on top. Add toppings – sliced jalapeños, shredded cheddar cheese, and chopped bacon.
4. Bake in a preheated oven at 350⁰ F for 35 minutes.

Nutri info per serving (4-inch square): 361 calories, 3g net carbs, 40g fat, 24g protein

MEXICAN CHEESE OMELET

Yield: 1 serving
Preparation time: 2 minutes
Cooking Time: 4 minutes

INGREDIENTS:

- Shredded Mexican blend cheese (organic)
- 1 tablespoon olive oil
- 2 eggs (organic)
- Salt and pepper to taste

DIRECTIONS:

1. Whisk eggs and half of the cheese in a bowl.
2. Grease pan with olive oil over low flame. Once heated, gently pour the egg mixture. Turn heat to medium and cook for 2 minutes. Turn it over, add the remaining cheese on top, and cook for 2 more minutes.
3. Transfer to a plate. Season with salt and pepper before serving.

Nutri info per serving (1 piece): 489 calories, 3g net carbs, 41g fat, 26g protein

CHICHARRONES WITH EGGS

Yield: 3 servings
Preparation time: 10 minutes
Cooking Time: 15 minutes

INGREDIENTS:

- 1/4 cup cilantro (chopped)
- 1/4 medium onion (diced)
- 2 medium jalapeño peppers (remove the seeds, diced)
- 1 medium avocado (cubed)
- 1 medium tomato (diced)
- Salt and pepper to taste
- 1.5 ounces pork rinds
- 5 eggs (whisked)
- 4 bacon slices

DIRECTIONS:

1. Cook the bacon slices on a pan over medium-high flame. Transfer to a plate and keep most of the grease on the pan.
2. Cook the pork rinds in the bacon grease until crispy. Turn the heat to medium and stir in the vegetables. Cook for 5 minutes and season to taste. Add cilantro and whisked eggs. Mix until the eggs are cooked.
3. Transfer to a plate. Add the avocado cubes and fold into the mixture. Top with crumbled bacon and your preferred toppings.

Nutri info per serving (1/3): 348.33 calories, 3.74g net carbs, 22.71g fat, 23.79g protein

CHORIZO SHAKSHUKA

Yield: 6 servings
Preparation time: 10 minutes
Cooking Time: 25 minutes

INGREDIENTS:

- 1/4 cup cilantro (chopped)
- 2 ounces queso fresco (crumbled)
- 6 large eggs
- 1 28-ounce can diced tomatoes (with juice)
- 1/4 teaspoon salt (adjust according to taste)
- 1/2 teaspoon black pepper
- 1/2 tablespoon ground cumin
- 1/2 tablespoon chili powder
- 1 tablespoon minced garlic
- 1 red bell pepper (diced)
- 1/2 cup diced onion
- 1 pound ground chorizo
- 1 tablespoon coconut oil

DIRECTIONS:

1. Heat coconut oil in a pan over medium flame. Once melted, cook the chorizo until browned or about 8 minutes. Transfer to a plate and set aside.
2. Sauté onion and bell pepper in the pan for 5 minutes. Stir in spices and minced garlic. Cook for a couple of minutes. Add tomatoes with the juice and the cooked chorizo. Mix well. Leave to simmer for 15 minutes. Use the back of a spoon to make 6 wells in the pan. Crack an egg into each hole. Cover the pan and cook for 6 to 10 minutes.
3. Transfer to a plate. Slice and top with chopped cilantro and crumbled queso fresco before serving.

Nutri info per serving (1/6): 504.17 calories, 6.98g net carbs, 38.86g fat, 29.19g protein

TACO SALAD

Yield: 6 servings
Preparation time: 5 minutes
Cooking Time: 10 minutes

INGREDIENTS:

- 1 cup sour cream
- 1 medium avocado (diced)
- 1 1/2 cups mozzarella cheese (pre-shredded)
- 2 small red tomatoes (chopped)
- 9 ounces iceberg lettuce (chopped)
- 8 ounces romaine lettuce (chopped)
- 1 teaspoon garlic powder
- 1 teaspoon dried parsley
- 1/2 teaspoon chili powder
- 1 teaspoon ground cumin
- 3/4 pound ground beef

DIRECTIONS:

1. Cook meat in a preheated pan over medium flame. Add spices and herbs. Stir until the meat is cooked through. Drain oil from the meat, transfer to a bowl and set aside.
2. In a salad bowl, put avocado, shredded mozzarella, tomatoes, and lettuce. Toss until combined. Top with sour cream and cooked ground beef.

Nutri info per serving (1 cup): 388.37 calories, 6.5g net carbs, 32.47g fat, 15.8g protein

CHICKEN ENCHILADA SERVED WITH GREEN CHILI SAUCE

Yield: 8 rolls
Preparation time: 25 minutes
Cooking Time: 35 minutes

INGREDIENTS:

- 1 head cabbage
- 2 7-ounce cans green chili
- 1 cup sour cream
- 1 cup chicken broth
- Salt and pepper to taste
- 1/2 teaspoon cumin
- 1/3 cup chopped cilantro
- 1 cup shredded cheese
- 4 green onions (chopped)
- 3 cups shredded chicken

DIRECTIONS:

1. Boil chicken broth in a saucepan over medium-high flame. Turn the heat to medium and add green chili and sour cream. Simmer until thick while stirring often.
2. Boil a pot of salted water. Carefully peel the cabbage leaves. Dip them in the salted water and dry on paper towels.
3. In a bowl, put cumin, cilantro, 3/4 of the shredded cheese, green, onion, salt, pepper, and shredded chicken. Mix well. Add mixture as filling to each of the cabbage leaf. Add a tablespoon of the sauce before rolling the leaves. Arrange the cabbage rolls in a baking dish.
4. Pour the remaining sauce on top of the cabbage rolls. Add the rest of the cheese on top. Bake in a preheated oven at 350 F for 30 minutes.

Nutri info per serving (1 roll): 240.5 calories, 7.82g net carbs, 13.96g fat, 18.4g protein

MEXICAN HASH FOR BREAKFAST

Yield: 2 servings
Preparation time: 10 minutes
Cooking Time: 20 minutes

INGREDIENTS:

- 1/2 cup diced avocado
- 2 large eggs
- 2 cups chopped chard
- 6 ounces Mexican chorizo (discard the casing)
- 1/2 cup chopped tomatoes
- 1 cup chopped zucchini
- Fresh cilantro (for garnishing)
- Salt and pepper to taste
- 1/2 cup green pepper (sliced)
- 1/2 small white or yellow onion (chopped)
- 1 tablespoon ghee

DIRECTIONS:

1. Put ghee in a heated pan over medium-high flame. Cook the green pepper and chopped onion for 3 minutes. Stir in chopped tomatoes and diced zucchini. Cook for 4 minutes while occasionally stirring. Add the chorizo and leave to cook for 5 minutes. Stir in the chard and cook for 3 minutes. Make 2 wells using the back of a spoon. Crack an egg in each hole. Season with salt and pepper.
2. Place the pan under the broiler. Cook for 5 minutes.
3. Top with fresh cilantro and diced avocado before serving.

Nutri info per serving (1/2): 452 calories, 7.5g net carbs, 34.9g fat, 22.8g protein

BREAKFAST TACOS

Yield: 3 servings
Preparation time: 10 minutes
Cooking Time: 30 minutes

INGREDIENTS:

- ounce cheddar cheese (shredded)
- 1/2 small avocado
- 3 bacon strips
- 2 tablespoons butter
- Salt and pepper to taste
- 6 large eggs
- 1 cup mozzarella cheese (shredded)

DIRECTIONS:

1. Put bacon in a tray lined with foil and cook in a preheated oven at 375^0 F for 20 minutes.
2. Preheat a pan over medium flame. Put 1/3 cup of mozzarella cheese and leave until browned. This will take about 3 minutes. Use tongs to get the cheese and drape it on a wooden spoon placed on sturdy material to form a shell. Repeat for the rest of the cheese.
3. Melt butter in a pan over medium flame. Cook scrambled eggs and season to taste.
4. Put bacon, avocado, and 1/3 of the cooked scrambled eggs to each shell. Top with cheddar cheese.

Nutri info per serving (1 taco): 443.67 calories, 2.38g net carbs, 35.68g fat, 26.41g protein

CHAPTER 4

MAIN DISH RECIPES

PULLED PORK MEXICAN STYLE

Yield: 6 servings
Preparation time: 45 minutes
Cooking Time: 30 minutes

INGREDIENTS:

- 1/4 cup water
- 1 1/2 lbs. boneless pork shoulder (sliced into 5)
- 1/2 teaspoon ground black pepper
- 1/2 teaspoon chili powder
- 1 teaspoon kosher salt
- 1 teaspoon garlic powder
- 1 teaspoon ground cumin
- 1 teaspoon onion powder
- 1 teaspoon smoked paprika
- 1 tablespoon Splenda or brown sugar

DIRECTIONS:

1. In a bowl, mix black pepper, chili powder, salt, paprika, onion powder, garlic powder, and brown sugar. Rub mixture all over the meat and leave to marinate for 30 minutes.
2. Place the marinated meat in the inner liner of your

pressure cooker. Put 1/4 cup of water at the pot's bottom. Cook for 25 minutes at high-temperature setting. Let it rest for 10 minutes after the timer's done before releasing the pressure.
3. Shred the cooked meat and top with your preferred fixings before serving.

Nutri info per serving (1/6): 157 calories, 3g net carbs, 4g fat, 25g protein

CHEESY GREEN CHILI BAKE WITH BEEF

Yield: 8 servings
Preparation time: 15 minutes
Cooking Time: 40 minutes

INGREDIENTS:

- 1/2 teaspoon ground chili powder
- 1/2 teaspoon ground cumin
- 1/2 cup sour cream (room temperature)
- 5 eggs
- 1 4-ounce can diced green chili (with juice)
- 1 small onion (chopped)
- 4 cups grated Mexican blend cheese
- Salt and pepper to taste
- 1 pound ground beef
- 4 teaspoons olive oil
- 1 27-ounce can green chili (roasted and peeled)

DIRECTIONS:

1. Put 2 teaspoons of olive oil in a pan over medium-high flame. Once heated, cook the meat while breaking it apart until browned. Season to taste and transfer to a plate.
2. Heat the remaining oil and cook the onion until soft. Add the diced green chili and juice. Cook for 3 minutes before adding the cooked meat. Cook for 3 more minutes.
3. Whisk the eggs in a bowl. Add chili powder, cumin, and sour cream. Whisk until combined.
4. Remove the seeds of the roasted green chili. Pat with paper towels to remove excess moisture. Put half of them in the bottom part of the casserole dish. Add half of the

cheese, meat, and egg mixture. Make another layer with the other half of the remaining ingredients.

5. Cover the dish with a foil. Bake in a preheated oven at 375⁰ F for 25 minutes.

6. Slice and serve with your preferred toppings.

Nutri info per serving (1/8): 461 calories, 5.5g net carbs, 34g fat, 33g protein

LOW CARB CHILI CON CARNE

Yield: 4 servings
Preparation time: 10 minutes
Cooking Time: 20 minutes

INGREDIENTS:

- 1 teaspoon cayenne pepper
- 1 28-ounce can diced tomatoes
- 1 cup tomato passata sauce
- 2 medium capsicums
- 1 onion (minced)
- 500 grams beef (minced)
- 4 bacon slices (chopped)

DIRECTIONS:

1. Fry the bacon slices in a pan over medium-high flame until crispy. Transfer to a plate. Add onion to the pan and cook in the bacon grease until browned. Stir in diced tomatoes and capsicums. Add tomato sauce and turn heat to low. Leave to simmer for 10 minutes.
2. Transfer to a bowl. Top with butter before serving.

Nutri info per serving (1/4): 371 calories, 8g net carbs, 26g fat, 23g protein

PORK CHOPS AL PASTOR

Yield: 4 servings
Preparation time: 10 minutes
Cooking Time: 8 minutes

INGREDIENTS:

- 1 tablespoon olive oil
- 1 tablespoon apple cider vinegar
- 1 teaspoon dried oregano leaves
- 1/2 teaspoon kosher salt
- 1/8 teaspoon ground cloves
- 1 teaspoon ground cumin
- 2 tablespoons canned chipotle peppers in adobo sauce
- 4 pork chops

For the butter

- 1 tablespoon lime zest
- 1 tablespoon fresh cilantro (minced)
- 1 teaspoon garlic (minced)
- 2 tablespoons red onion (minced)
- 1/4 cup pineapple (chopped)
- 1 tablespoon granulated Erythritol (optional)
- 1/2 cup salted butter (room temperature)

DIRECTIONS:

1. Put oil, vinegar, salt, oregano, cloves, cumin, and chipotle peppers in a blender. Process until smooth.
2. Cover meat with the marinade. Leave in the fridge for at least 2 hours or overnight. Leave at room temperature for 30 minutes before cooking.

3. Cook meat in a preheated grill at 400⁰ F for 3 minutes. Turn over and cook for 3 more minutes. Transfer to a platter.

4. Put all ingredients for the butter in a bowl and mix well. Top each cooked meat with the mixture.

Nutri info per serving (1 pork chop, plus 2 tablespoons butter): 495 calories, 1g net carbs, 47g fat, 25g protein

ALL-DAY MEXICAN BOWL

Yield: 2 servings
Preparation time: 15 minutes
Cooking Time: 15 minutes

INGREDIENTS:

- 1 tablespoon extra-virgin olive oil
- 1 medium spring onion (sliced)
- 1/2 red bell pepper (chopped)
- 1/2 cup cherry tomatoes (halved)
- 1 small yellow onion (diced)
- 1 tablespoon fresh oregano
- 1/2 jalapeño pepper
- 2 Italian style sausages (gluten-free, remove casing)
- 2 Mexican chorizo sausages (remove casing)
- Salt and pepper to taste
- 1/4 teaspoon paprika
- 1/2 avocado (diced)
- 2 large eggs (poached)
- 1 tablespoon chopped fresh coriander
- 1 teaspoon fresh lime juice
- 1/4 teaspoon coconut aminos

DIRECTIONS:

1. Put meat in a pan over medium-low flame and fry for 5 minutes as you break them apart. Stir in jalapeño, paprika, and onion. Cook for 8 minutes. Set aside.
2. Put coconut aminos in a bowl. Add lime, olive oil, pepper, salt, spring onion, red pepper, oregano, and tomatoes. Toss until combined.

3. Put meat in a bowl. Top with avocado, poached egg, sriracha sauce, chopped coriander, and sour cream.

Nutri info per serving (1 cup): 726 calories, 7.9g net carbs, 60g fat, 32.5g protein

CHORI POLLO

Yield: 6 servings
Preparation time: 10 minutes
Cooking Time: 20 minutes

INGREDIENTS:

- 1 cup shredded Monterey jack cheese
- 1/2 teaspoon chipotle powder
- 1/2 teaspoon garlic powder
- 1/2 teaspoon ground cumin
- 1/2 teaspoon ground coriander
- 8 ounces Mexican chorizo (raw)
- 3 cups shredded chicken (cooked)
- 2 tablespoons butter
- 1 cup sliced onions

DIRECTIONS:

1. Put butter in a pan over medium-low flame. Cook the onions for 10 minutes or until caramelized. Add salt and pepper. Transfer to a plate and set aside.
2. Cook the chorizo for 5 minutes while breaking it apart. Transfer to a bowl.
3. Put the shredded chicken in the pan. Add chipotle powder, garlic powder, cumin, and coriander. Season to taste and cook for 5 minutes. Transfer to a casserole dish and spread out evenly. Add chorizo and top with onions. Sprinkle with shredded cheese. Bake in a preheated oven at 375 degrees for 10 minutes.

Nutri info per serving (3/4 cup): 405 calories, 3g net carbs, 30g fat, 37g protein

MEXICAN EMPANADAS

Yield: 8 servings
Preparation time: 20 minutes
Cooking Time: 30 minutes

INGREDIENTS:

- Pie crust (keto-friendly and gluten-free)
- 1/2 cup green olives (pitted, rinsed, and halved lengthwise)
- 1/2 teaspoon sweetener of choice
- 1/2 cup chicken broth
- 1/8 teaspoon cayenne pepper
- 1 teaspoon dried oregano
- 2 teaspoons paprika
- 1 tablespoon ground cumin
- Freshly ground black pepper to taste
- Kosher salt to taste
- 1 red bell pepper (deseeded and chopped)
- 1/3 onion (minced)
- 1 egg (lightly beaten for egg wash)
- 1/2 pound ground beef
- Extra-virgin olive oil for cooking

DIRECTIONS:

1. Put olive oil in a pan over high flame. Add beef once heated and break it up as you cook. Transfer to a bowl while leaving the grease to the pan.
2. Turn heat to medium and add bell pepper and onion. Cook for 8 minutes while stirring often. Add pepper, salt, cayenne, oregano, paprika, and cumin. Cook for a minute. Put back the cooked meat and add chicken broth. Add sugar and season to taste. Simmer for 20 minutes. Transfer

to a bowl and let it cool. Cover the bowl and leave in the fridge for 3 hours.

3. Cut the pie crust dough into 8. Add 3 tablespoons of the filling before folding the crust and sealing its edges. Arrange the empanadas in a baking tray lined with mat. Brush top with the egg wash. Bake for 15 minutes in a preheated oven at 375 F. Flip them over and continue baking for 15 more minutes.

Nutri info per serving (1 empanada): 230 calories, 3g net carbs, 19g fat, 6g protein

LETTUCE WRAP TACOS WITH TURKEY

Yield: 10 tacos
Preparation time: 8 minutes
Cooking Time: 8 minutes

INGREDIENTS:

For the tacos

- 2 iceberg lettuce heads
- 2 tablespoons fresh lime juice
- 1 cup chopped cilantro
- 1/2 cup green onions (thinly sliced)
- Salt to taste
- 2 pounds ground turkey
- 1/4 teaspoon ground chipotle pepper
- 1 1/2 teaspoons ground cumin
- 1 4-ounce can diced green chili
- 1 teaspoon minced garlic
- 2 teaspoons olive oil

For the salsa

- 2 tablespoons fresh lime juice
- 1/4 cup finely chopped cilantro
- 1 cup finely chopped cherry tomatoes
- 2 medium avocados (diced)
- Sea salt to taste
- 2 tablespoons olive oil (optional)

DIRECTIONS:

1. Put olive oil in a pan over medium-high flame. Once heated, cook green chili and minced garlic for a minute. Stir in ground chipotle pepper and cumin. Continue cooking for a minute. Add the meat and season with salt. Break the meat as you stir. Cook until lightly browned.

Add the onions and cook for a couple of minutes. Remove from heat. Add 2 tablespoons of lime juice and a cup of chopped cilantro.

2. Prepare the salsa. Put the diced avocado in a bowl. Add lime juice, olive oil, chopped cilantro, and chopped tomato. Season to taste.

3. Chop off the end part of the lettuce and remove the core. Cut into 4 and remove outer leaves. They will serve as the cups for the taco meat.

4. Add 3 tablespoons of the turkey mixture to each lettuce cup. Add salsa on top before serving.

Nutri info per serving (1 taco): 358 calories, 5g net carbs, 26g fat, 25g protein

PORK RIND TORTILLAS WITH STEAK TACOS

Yield: 6 mini tortillas
Preparation time: 15 minutes
Cooking Time: 15 minutes

INGREDIENTS:

- 2 6-ounce top sirloin steaks
- 2 tablespoons cream cheese
- 1 egg
- 3/4 cup mozzarella cheese
- 1 cup crushed pork rinds
- Toppings of choice

DIRECTIONS:

1. Put pork rinds in a food processor and process until chopped and crumbled.
2. Place cream cheese and mozzarella in a heatproof bowl. Microwave for 30 seconds. Mix until combined.
3. Place pork rind in a mixing bowl. Add egg and cheese mixture. Mix using your hands. Form the mixture into a ball and put it in between two parchment paper. Roll out until thin. Cut it out into circles. Cook in a pan over medium flame until browned.
4. Bring steak to room temperature. Season to taste.
5. Put oil in a pan over medium flame. Once heated, cook steak until all sides are seared. Transfer to a plate and leave to rest for 10 minutes. Slice and place on top of the pork rind tortillas. Add toppings of choice before serving.

Nutri info per serving (1 mini tortilla): 97 calories, 1g net carbs, 7g fat, 7g protein

CORNBREAD CASSEROLE TACO PIE

Yield: 8 servings
Preparation time: 15 minutes
Cooking Time: 35 minutes

INGREDIENTS:

For the cornbread base

- 1 tablespoon baking powder
- 3 large eggs
- 2 ounces cream cheese (heat in the microwave until soft)
- 1/4 teaspoon sweet corn extract (optional)
- 2 cups almond flour
- 1 cups part skim mozzarella cheese (shredded)

For the ground beef taco meat

- 1 cup cheddar cheese (divided)
- Salt and pepper to taste
- 1/2 cup beef broth
- 2 tablespoons tomato paste
- 2 tablespoons homemade taco seasoning
- 1 pound lean ground beef

DIRECTIONS:

1. Cook ground beef in a pan over medium flame. Break up the meat as you cook. Add beef broth, tomato paste, and taco seasoning. Cook until most of the liquid is absorbed. Season to taste. Remove from the stove, add half of the cheese and stir.
2. Prepare the cornbread base. Put corn extract, baking powder, almond flour, eggs, and cheeses in a food

processor. Process until combined and thick. Transfer to a greased iron skillet and spread evenly. Put the taco meat on top. Bake in a preheated oven at 350 F for 40 minutes. Put the rest of the cheese and place in the oven until melted.

Nutri info per serving (1 slice): 436 calories, 5g net carbs, 30g fat, 31g protein

PAN STEAK FAJITAS

Yield: 5 servings
Preparation time: 5 minutes
Cooking Time: 15 minutes

INGREDIENTS:

- 1 yellow pepper (sliced)
- 1 red pepper (sliced)
- 750 grams steak
- 1 lemon juice and zest
- 1 lime juice and zest
- 60 ml coconut oil
- Salt and pepper to taste
- 1 tablespoon ground cumin powder
- 1/2 teaspoon chili powder
- 1 onion (thinly sliced)
- 2 garlic cloves (crushed)

DIRECTIONS:

1. Put all the ingredients in a baking tray. Bake in a preheated oven at 350^0 F for 10 minutes. Stir and continue baking for 5 more minutes. You can serve this along with green salad or coleslaw with olive oil or lime dressing.

Nutri info per serving (1 cup): 440 calories, 4 g net carbs, 33g fat, 31g protein

TACO-FLAVORED SHREDDED PORK

Yield: 10 servings
Preparation time: 10 minutes
Cooking Time: 10 hours

INGREDIENTS:

- Homemade taco seasoning
- 1/4 cup grass-fed butter (or ghee)
- 4 pounds pork roast
- 2 cups chicken stock
-

DIRECTIONS:

1. Put butter, pork roast, taco seasoning, and chicken stock in a preheated slow cooker at low setting. Cover and leave to cook for 10 hours.
2. Shred meat using two forks.

Nutri info per serving (1 cup): 411.1 calories, 1.6g net carbs, 11.3g fat, 33g protein

TACO CABBAGE SKILLET

Yield: 4 servings
Preparation time: 5 minutes
Cooking Time: 10 minutes

INGREDIENTS:

- 3/4 cup cheese (shredded)
- 2 teaspoons chili powder
- 2 cups shredded cabbage
- Salt and pepper to taste
- 1/2 cup salsa
- 1 pound ground beef
- Green onions and sour cream for garnishing (optional)

DIRECTIONS:

1. Cook meat in a pan over medium-high flame until browned. Discard the fat. Add cabbage, seasoning, and salsa. Cook until it boils. Turn the heat to medium and cover the pan. Cook for 12 minutes and remove from heat. Stir in the cheese until melted.
2. Add your preferred garnishing before serving.

Nutri info per serving (1/4): 325 calories, 4g net carbs, 21g fat, 30g protein

LETTUCE WRAPS WITH CHICKEN TACO

Yield: 4 servings
Preparation time: 15 minutes
Cooking Time: 15 minutes

INGREDIENTS:

- 1 tablespoon olive oil
- 2 garlic cloves (minced)
- 2 tablespoons chili powder
- 1 pound chicken breasts or thighs (boneless and skinless)

For the cilantro sauce

- A pinch of salt
- 1/2 lime (juiced)
- 1 garlic clove (minced)
- 2 tablespoons olive oil
- 1/2 cup Greek yogurt
- 1/2 cup loosely packed cilantro

For the assembly

- 1/4 cup onion (diced)
- 1 tomato (diced)
- 1 avocado (diced)
- 8 Romaine lettuce leaves (rinsed)

DIRECTIONS:

1. Put chicken in a bowl. Add spices, olive oil, and garlic. Leave in the fridge for at least 30 minutes or overnight to marinate.
2. Discard the marinade and cook the meat on a grill over medium-high flame. Cook each side for 10 minutes.
3. Prepare the sauce. Put all the ingredients for the sauce in a blender and process for a minute.

4. Put chicken in each lettuce wrap. Add avocado, onion, and tomatoes. Top with taco or cilantro sauce.

Nutri info per serving (1 taco): 161 calories, 4.9g net carbs, 9.1g fat, 14.5g protein

ZUCCHINI CHICKEN ENCHILADA

Yield: 12 servings
Preparation time: 15 minutes
Cooking Time: 25 minutes

INGREDIENTS:

- 1 cup shredded cheddar cheese
- 1 cup shredded Monterey Jack cheese
- 4 large zucchini (thinly sliced)
- 1 1/3 cups red enchilada sauce (divided)
- 3 cups shredded chicken (free-range, organic)
- 2 teaspoons chili powder
- 1 teaspoon ground cumin
- 2 garlic cloves (minced)
- Salt and black pepper to taste
- 1 large onion (chopped)
- 1 tablespoon extra-virgin olive oil
- Sour cream and cilantro leaves for garnishing

DIRECTIONS:

1. Put oil in a pan over medium flame. Cook onion for 5 minutes. Add salt, 1 cup enchilada sauce, shredded chicken, chili powder, cumin, and garlic. Mix well.
2. Arrange 4 zucchini slices in an overlapping manner. Place 2 tablespoons of the chicken mixture. Gently roll the zucchini slices and arrange on a baking dish. Pour the rest of the enchilada sauce on top of the zucchini rolls. Add shredded cheeses on top. Bake in a preheated oven at 350 degrees for 20 minutes.
3. Add garnishing before serving.

Nutri info per serving (1/12): 154 calories, 4.4g net carbs, 7.2g fat, 16.7g protein

GREEN ENCHILADA MEATBALLS

Yield: 16 meatballs
Preparation time: 5 minutes
Cooking Time: 15 minutes

INGREDIENTS:

- 1/4 cup crumbled queso fresco
- 1 teaspoon garlic powder
- 1 tablespoon ground coriander
- 1 tablespoon ground cumin
- 2 tablespoons green onions (chopped)
- 1 tablespoon cilantro (chopped)
- Oil for frying
- 1/4 teaspoon black pepper
- 1/2 teaspoon salt
- 1/4 cup almond flour
- 1 egg
- 1 pound ground chicken or turkey
- *To serve*
- 1/4 cup crumbled queso fresco
- 1/2 cup salsa verde

DIRECTIONS:

1. Put all ingredients for the meatballs in a bowl and mix until combined. Divide into 16, and shape them into balls.
2. Heat oil in a pan over medium-high flame. Cook the meatballs until browned. Transfer to a plate and set aside.
3. Put 2 tablespoons of salsa verde on the bottom of a platter. Arrange the meatballs on top, and drizzle with the remaining salsa. Sprinkle crumbled cheese on top.

Nutri info per serving (4 meatballs): 341 calories, 28g fat, 3.4g net carbs, 32g protein

CHICKEN ENCHILADA CASSEROLE

Yield: 8 servings
Preparation time: 20 minutes
Cooking Time: 40 minutes

INGREDIENTS:

For the base

- 2 eggs (whisked)
- 1/2 teaspoon oregano
- 1 teaspoon smoked paprika
- 1/4 teaspoon salt
- 1/2 teaspoon cumin
- 1/2 teaspoon chili powder
- 1/4 cup coconut flour
- 6 cups cauliflower florets (steamed)

For the top layer

- 2 cups Mexican shredded cheese
- 10 ounces enchilada sauce
- 1/2 teaspoon oregano
- 1 teaspoon smoked paprika
- 1/4 teaspoon salt
- 1/2 teaspoon cumin
- 1/2 teaspoon chili powder
- 1 1/2 pounds cooked chicken shredded
- Toppings of choice

DIRECTIONS:

1. Put the steamed cauliflower florets in a food processor. Process until the mixture resembles rice. Add spices and flour. Process until combined. Transfer to a bowl. Add the eggs and mix well.
2. Mix the spices and shredded chicken in a bowl.
3. Put the cauliflower base on a baking tray. Spread all over.

Add the chicken mixture on top, and drizzle with enchilada sauce. Sprinkle shredded cheese on top. Cover and bake in a preheated oven at 350⁰ degrees for 30 minutes. Remove the cover and bake for 10 more minutes.

4. Slice and serve.

Nutri info per serving (1/8): 357 calories, 6g net carbs, 21g fat, 31g protein

SPAGHETTI SQUASH TACO BOWL

Yield: 4 servings
Preparation time: 20 minutes
Cooking Time: 1 hour

INGREDIENTS:

- 1 teaspoon chili powder
- 2 teaspoons olive oil
- 1 large spaghetti squash (cut into fourths lengthwise, deseeded)
- Freshly ground black pepper to taste
- 1 teaspoon Spike seasoning

For the ground beef

- 2 cups water
- 1 4-ounce can diced green chili with juice
- 2 tablespoons taco seasoning
- 1 teaspoon Spike seasoning
- 1 pound lean ground beef
- 1 medium onion (chopped)
- 2 teaspoons olive oil

Toppings

- 1 cup grated cheese
- 1 cup chopped cherry tomatoes
- 1 tablespoon freshly squeezed lime juice
- 1 medium avocado (chopped)
- 1 6-ounce can olives (drained and sliced in half lengthwise)
- Salsa and sour cream (optional)

DIRECTIONS:

1. Brush the squash with olive oil and season with black pepper, Spike seasoning, and chili powder. Roast in a preheated oven at 400⁰ F for an hour.
2. Heat a teaspoon of olive oil in a pan over medium-high flame. Add onion and cook until browned. Add the ground beef and break apart as you cook. Add taco and Spike seasoning. Cook until browned. Turn heat to low. Add 2 cups of water and diced green chili with juice. Simmer until most of the water is removed.
3. In a bowl, put avocados, olives, tomatoes, and lime juice. Toss until combined.
4. Leave the cooked squash until cool. Scrape with a fork to discard the skin. Divide into 4 bowls. Top each with the cheese, meat and avocado mixture. Add salsa and sour cream before serving.

Nutri info per serving (1/4): 416 calories, 13.8g net carbs, 26g fat, 29g protein

CARNE ASADA WITH CHIMICHURRI SAUCE

Yield: 4 servings
Preparation time: 5 minutes
Cooking Time: 10 minutes

INGREDIENTS:

- 1 teaspoon salt
- 1/2 teaspoon ground black pepper
- 1/2 teaspoon cayenne pepper
- 2 tablespoons chopped cilantro
- 1 teaspoon dried oregano leaves
- 1 teaspoon ground cumin
- 1 teaspoon minced garlic
- 1 tablespoon apple cider vinegar
- 2 tablespoons avocado oil
- 1 tablespoon lime juice
- 1 pound flank or skirt steak

For the sauce

- 1/2 teaspoon salt
- 1/4 cup red wine vinegar
- 1 teaspoon red pepper flakes
- 1 teaspoon dried oregano
- 1 teaspoon lemon zest
- 1/3 cup olive oil
- 4 garlic cloves (chopped)
- 1/2 cup parsley (chopped)

DIRECTIONS:

1. In a bowl, put salt, black pepper, cayenne, cilantro, oregano, cumin, garlic, cider vinegar, avocado oil, and lime juice. Mix until combined. Put the steak and leave to marinate for at least 2 hours or overnight.

2. Leave the marinated meat at room temperature half an hour before cooking. Grill each side of the meat over direct heat for 5 minutes. Transfer to a plate and leave to rest for 10 minutes.
3. Slice and serve with chimichurri sauce.
4. To make the sauce, put all ingredients in a blender. Process for 20 seconds.

Nutri info per serving (4 ounces steak, 2 tablespoons sauce): 330 calories, 0g net carbs, 23g fat, 24g protein

CHAPTER 5

SOUP RECIPES

CHICKEN ENCHILADA HOT DISH

Yield: 4 servings
Preparation time: 10 minutes
Cooking Time: 50 minutes

INGREDIENTS:

- 1/2 medium lime (juiced)
- 6 ounces chicken (shredded)
- 8 ounces cream cheese
- 4 cups chicken broth
- 1/2 teaspoon cayenne pepper
- 1 teaspoon chili powder
- 1 teaspoon oregano
- 2 teaspoons cumin
- 1 cup tomatoes (diced)
- Salt and pepper to taste
- 3 tablespoons olive oil
- 1/2 cup cilantro (chopped)
- 2 teaspoons minced garlic
- 1 medium red bell pepper (diced)
- 3 celery stalks (diced)

DIRECTIONS:

1. Put oil in a pan over medium-high flame. Once heated, cook bell peppers, garlic, and celery for 3 minutes. Stir in the spices. Add cilantro and chicken broth. Turn heat to low and leave to simmer for 20 minutes. Stir in cream

cheese and bring to another boil. Leave to simmer for 25 minutes. Add shredded chicken and lime juice.

2. Sprinkle with cheese, cilantro, or sour cream before serving.

Nutri info per serving (1 1/2 cups): 365.5 calories, 8.58g net carbs, 33.64g fat, 16.8g protein

LOW CARB CHILI SOUP

Yield: 4 servings
Preparation time: 10 minutes
Cooking Time: 20 minutes

INGREDIENTS:

- 4 tablespoons fresh cilantro (chopped)
- 2 ounces queso fresco
- 1 medium avocado
- 2 tablespoons butter
- 16 ounces chicken thighs (chopped)
- 4 tablespoons tomato paste
- 1/2 teaspoon ground cumin
- Salt and pepper to taste
- 1/2 lime (juiced)
- 1 teaspoon turmeric
- 2 cups water
- 2 cups chicken broth
- 2 medium chili peppers (sliced)
- 2 tablespoons olive oil
- 1 teaspoon coriander seeds

DIRECTIONS:

1. Put oil in a pan over medium-high flame. Once heated, cook meat until browned. Set aside.
2. Put 2 tablespoons of olive oil in a pan over medium flame. Add the coriander seeds and cook until fragrant. Season with sliced chili. Turn heat to low. Add water and leave to simmer. Season to taste. Stir in butter and tomato paste. Simmer for 10 minutes. Add lime juice.
3. Divide meat into 4 bowls. Add soup and garnish with cilantro, queso fresco, and 1/4 of an avocado.

Nutri info per serving (1/4): 369.5 calories, 6.44g net carbs, 25.86g fat, 27.03g protein

PRESSURE COOKER KING RANCH CHICKEN SOUP

Yield: 8 servings
Preparation time: 15 minutes
Cooking Time: 15 minutes

INGREDIENTS:

- 2 cups shredded Mexican blend cheese
- 1 1/2 teaspoons xanthan gum
- 1/2 cup heavy whipping cream
- 1 medium jalapeno (diced, deseeded)
- 1 10-ounce can tomatoes (diced) with green chilies
- 2.5 pounds chicken breasts (boneless and skinless)
- 1 teaspoon salt
- 1 tablespoon garlic powder
- Chopped cilantro to taste
- Pepper to taste
- 1 tablespoon ground cumin
- 4 teaspoons chili powder
- 4 cups chicken broth
- 1/2 cup coconut flour
- 8 tablespoons butter

DIRECTIONS:

1. Set your pressure cooker to sautés. Put butter and coconut flour. Stir for 3 minutes. Add chicken broth, pepper, salt, garlic powder, ground cumin, and chili powder. Add meat, jalapeno, and green chili. Close the lid and cook on a high-temperature setting for 15 minutes. Perform a manual release once done.
2. Add xanthan gum and whipping cream. Mix well. Stir in the cheese.
3. Top with cheese and chopped cilantro before serving.

Nutri info per serving (1 cup): 463.13 calories, 4.62g net carbs, 29.84g fat, 41.22g protein

TASTY CHICKEN FAJITA SOUP

Yield: 14 servings
Preparation time: 20 minutes
Cooking Time: 7 hours

INGREDIENTS:

- 4 large garlic cloves (minced)
- 6 ounces mushrooms (thinly sliced)
- 1 medium onion (diced)
- 1 medium orange bell pepper (diced)
- 1 medium yellow bell pepper (diced)
- 1 14.5-ounce can diced tomatoes
- 32 ounces chicken stock
- 1 1/2 pounds chicken breast
- 2 teaspoons sea salt
- 2 tablespoons fresh cilantro (chopped)
- 4 tablespoons Taco seasoning

DIRECTIONS:

1. Put all ingredients in a slow cooker. Close the lid and cook for 6 hours on low setting. Shred meat and continue cooking for 1 hour.

Nutri info per serving (1 cup): 73 calories, 4g net carbs, 1.5g fat, 12g protein

LOW CARB JALAPENO POPPER SOUP

Yield: 4 servings
Preparation time: 5 minutes
Cooking Time: 20 minutes

INGREDIENTS:

- 4 large jalapeno peppers (rinsed and grilled)
- 3/4 cup Monterey jack cheese (shredded)
- 3/4 cup sharp cheddar cheese (shredded)
- 1/2 teaspoon garlic powder
- 2 tablespoon salsa verde
- 2 cups water or chicken broth
- 1/4 teaspoon xanthan gum (optional)
- 1/2 cup heavy cream
- 4 ounces cream cheese
- 4 raw bacon slices

DIRECTIONS:

1. Fry bacon in a pan over medium flame until crisp. Set aside.
2. Add water or broth, cream cheese, and heavy cream to the grease in the pan. Simmer until smooth. Add shredded cheese, salsa verde, and garlic powder.
3. Remove the seeds and skins of the jalapeno before mincing. Put them into the soup and simmer for 5 minutes. Season to taste. If you want the sauce to be thicker, you can stir in the xanthan gum.
4. Garnish with chopped bacon before serving.

Nutri info per serving (1 cup): 425 calories, 2.5g net carbs, 38g fat, 17g protein

TACO SOUP WITH TURKEY

Yield: 15 servings
Preparation time: 30 minutes
Cooking Time: 6 hours

INGREDIENTS:

- 1 cup heavy cream
- 8 ounces cream cheese (room temperature)
- 1 1/2 teaspoons sea salt
- 1 teaspoon chili powder
- 2 tablespoons cumin
- 3/4 cup sweet onion (diced)
- 20 ounces ground turkey
- 3 garlic cloves (minced)
- 4 cups beef broth
- 1 10-ounce can diced tomatoes and green chili
- 1 14.5-ounce can Mexican seasoned stewed tomatoes
- 1 15-ounce can black beans (drained)

DIRECTIONS:

1. Put garlic, beef broth, tomatoes and chili with juice, stewed tomatoes with juice, and black beans in a slow cooker. Close the lid and cook on low setting.
2. Put oil in a pan over medium-high flame. Once heated, add sea salt, chili powder, onion, and ground turkey. Cook for 15 minutes as you stir. Turn heat to low. Add cream cheese. Mix well.
3. Transfer the meat mixture to the slow cooker. Stir and cover the lid. Cook for 6 hours.

Nutri info per serving (1 cup): 178 calories, 6g net carbs, 10g fat, 4.5g protein

GREEN CHICKEN ENCHILADA HOT DISH

Yield: 4 servings
Preparation time: 5 minutes
Cooking Time: 10 minutes

INGREDIENTS:

- 2 cups chicken (cooked and shredded)
- 2 cups bone broth or chicken stock
- 1 cup sharp cheddar cheese (shredded)
- 4 ounces cream cheese (room temperature)
- 1/2 cup salsa verde

DIRECTIONS:

1. Put chicken stock, cheddar cheese, cream cheese, and salsa in a blender. Process until smooth. Transfer to a pan over medium flame. Cook for a couple of minutes. Add shredded chicken and cook for 5 minutes.
2. Top with cilantro and shredded cheddar cheese before serving.

Nutri info per serving (1 1/2 cups): 346 calories, 3g net carbs, 22g fat, 32g protein

CHICKEN TACO SOUP WITH CABBAGE

Yield: 4 servings
Preparation time: 10 minutes
Cooking Time: 15 minutes

INGREDIENTS:

- 2 cups chicken stock
- 1 teaspoon red chili flakes (optional)
- 1/4 cup celery (chopped)
- Lemon wedges
- 1/2 cup fresh coriander leaves for garnishing
- 1/2 cup sharp cheddar cheese
- Salt to taste
- 2 teaspoons dried oregano
- 1 tablespoon roasted cumin powder
- 1/2 tablespoon chipotle chili powder
- 1/2 tablespoon red chili powder
- 1 cup plum tomato (blanched and chopped)
- 1 medium red bell pepper (chopped)
- 2 cups shredded cabbage
- 300 grams chicken breast (boneless and skinless, chunked)
- 1 medium onion (chopped)
- 1 tablespoon garlic (minced)
- 1 tablespoon vegetable oil

DIRECTIONS:

1. Put oil in a pan over medium-high flame. Cook garlic until lightly browned. Stir in the onions and cook until soft. Add meat and celery. Cook for a minute. Stir in shredded cabbage and red bell pepper. Cook for 2 minutes. Add tomatoes and spices. Mix well. Cook for 2 more minutes before. Add the stock and season to taste. Cover and bring to a boil.

2. Garnish soup with cheese, lemon wedges, and coriander
    leaves before serving.

*Nutri info per serving (1 cup): 285 calories, 14g net carbs, 12g fat,
25g protein*

CREAMY TACO SOUP

Yield: 20 cups
Preparation time: 5 minutes
Cooking Time: 25 minutes

INGREDIENTS:

- 16 ounces cream cheese
- 6 ounces chopped chilies
- 1 pound of your preferred fresh or frozen veggies
- 1 bell pepper (chopped)
- 1 large onion (chopped)
- 2 pounds ground beef
- 2 tablespoons lime juice
- 4 cups homemade chicken stock
- 48 ounces diced tomatoes
- 1 tablespoon chopped garlic
- 1/4 cup Taco seasoning, plus more for serving

For the homemade taco seasoning

- 2 teaspoons black pepper
- 2 teaspoons sea or pink salt
- 1 tablespoon ground cumin
- 1 teaspoon paprika
- 2 teaspoons dried oregano
- 1/2 teaspoon crushed red pepper flakes
- 2 teaspoons onion powder
- 2 teaspoons garlic powder
- 2 tablespoons chili powder

DIRECTIONS:

1. Set your pressure cooker to sauté. Put oil and cook meat until browned. Add the rest of the ingredients. Mix well. Close the lid and pressure cook for 25 minutes on a high setting. Perform manual pressure release.

2. Season to taste. Stir in cream cheese until melted.

Nutri info per serving (1 cup): 177 calories, 5.5g net carbs, 8g fat, 17g protein

SOPA DE LIMA WITH CHICKEN

Yield: 4 servings
Preparation time: 25 minutes
Cooking Time: 20 minutes

INGREDIENTS:

- 1 avocado (chopped)
- 2 tablespoons fresh cilantro (chopped)
- 1/2 teaspoon lime zest (optional)
- 1/3 cup lime juice
- 1 tablespoon olive oil
- 1/2 onion (chopped)
- 2 tomatoes (chopped)
- 4 garlic cloves (minced)
- 2 Serrano chili peppers (deseeded and chopped)
- 4 cups organic chicken broth
- 1/4 teaspoon garlic powder
- 1/4 teaspoon chili powder
- 4 chicken breast halves
- A dash of sea salt (optional)

DIRECTIONS:

1. Put meat on a greased baking dish. Add garlic powder and chili powder. Bake in a preheated oven at 400^0 F for 20 minutes.
2. Put olive oil in a pot over medium flame. Once heated, sauté onion, peppers, and garlic for 3 minutes. Add tomatoes and cook for 2 minutes. Add lime juice and broth. Turn heat to low and simmer for 5 minutes. Stir in the baked chicken. Reduce heat to medium and wait until it boils. Turn heat to low and leave to simmer for 20 minutes.

3. Transfer to serving bowls. Top with avocado chunks and
    cilantro. Season to taste.

*Nutri info per serving (1 cup): 174 calories, 7g net carbs, 11.5g fat,
7.1g protein*

CHAPTER 6

RECIPES FOR DESSERTS AND DRINKS

MEXICAN HOT CHOCOLATE COOKIES

Yield: 15 cookies
Preparation time: 5 minutes
Cooking Time: 15 minutes

INGREDIENTS:

- 1/2 teaspoon cayenne pepper
- 2 1/2 teaspoons cinnamon
- 1 1/2 teaspoons chili powder
- 1/2 cup Splenda
- 8 tablespoons cocoa powder (unsweetened)
- 1/4 teaspoon salt
- 2 teaspoons vanilla
- 4 large eggs
- 3 tablespoons salted butter
- 1/2 cup coconut oil
- 3/4 cup coconut flour

DIRECTIONS:

1. Put coconut flour, Splenda, salt, cayenne pepper, chili powder, and cocoa powder in a bowl. Mix until combined.
2. Microwave butter and coconut oil for 15 seconds. Mix well.
3. Add vanilla, eggs, and butter mixture to the flour mixture.

Mix until combined. Shape the dough into cookies. Arrange them on a baking pan. Bake in a preheated oven at 350⁰ F for 15 minutes.

Nutri info per serving (1 cookie): 134.33 calories, 1.41g net carbs, 12.42g fat, 3.13g protein

KETO FLAN

Yield: 4 servings
Preparation time: 10 minutes
Cooking Time: 30 minutes

INGREDIENTS:

- 1/4 cup Erythritol (for the custard)
- 1/3 cup Erythritol (for the caramel)
- 1 tablespoon vanilla
- 2 large egg yolks
- 2 large eggs
- 1 cup heavy whipping cream
- 1 tablespoon butter
- 1/8 cup water

DIRECTIONS:

1. Prepare the caramel. Put Erythritol in a pan over medium flame while stirring often. Add butter and water. Cook until golden brown while occasionally stirring. Spoon caramel to each ramekin. Set aside.
2. Put whipping cream, vanilla, and Erythritol in a bowl. Whisk until combined. Gradually add the eggs. Mix well. Put mixture to each ramekin.
3. Arrange the ramekins in a casserole dish. Add water and bake for 30 minutes at 350 F. Take them out of the oven and leave to rest in the hot water for 10 minutes.
4. Place in the fridge for 4 hours or overnight before serving.

Nutri info per serving (1 ramekin): 298 calories, 2.4g net carbs, 31.5g fat, 4.5g protein

SOPAPILLA CHEESECAKE

Yield: 10 servings
Preparation time: 10 minutes
Cooking Time: 30 minutes

INGREDIENTS:

- 2 teaspoons vanilla extract
- 1/3 cup Swerve confectioners
- 2 8-ounce package cream cheese (room temperature)
- 2 tablespoons granulated Erythritol (mixed with 1 tablespoon cinnamon)
- 4 tablespoons melted butter
- 1 1/4 cups water
- 5 large eggs
- 1 4-ounce bag pork rinds (snack-style)

DIRECTIONS:

1. Put pork rind in a food processor. Process until powdered. Transfer to a bowl. Add water and 3 eggs. Whisk until combined.
2. Put 2 tablespoons of butter in a pan over medium flame. Cook a big scoop of the batter at a time. Spread it out evenly and cook until browned around the edges. Continue cooking until you have 4 tortillas.
3. Place one tortilla on a greased pie pan. Use 2 pieces to cover the edges. Brush top with melted butter. Add Erythritol and cinnamon mixture. Bake in a preheated oven at 350⁰ F for 10 minutes.
4. Put cream cheese, vanilla extract, 2 eggs, and Swerve

confectioners in a bowl. Mix well. Put on top of the crust and spread evenly. Slice the remaining batter into wedges and place on top. Add Erythritol and cinnamon mixture on top. Continue baking for 20 minutes.

5. Allow to cool before slicing.

Nutri info per serving (1/10): 293.8 calories, 3.01g net carbs, 26g fat, 11.44g protein

CHURRO MUG CAKE

Yield: 1 serving
Preparation time:
Cooking Time:

INGREDIENTS:

For the base

- 1/2 teaspoon baking powder
- 7 drops liquid Stevia
- 1 tablespoon Erythritol
- 2 tablespoons almond flour
- 2 tablespoons butter
- 1 large egg

For flavoring

- 1/8 teaspoon allspice
- 1/8 teaspoon ginger
- 1/4 teaspoon vanilla
- 1/4 teaspoon nutmeg
- 1/4 teaspoon cinnamon
- 2 tablespoons almond flour

DIRECTIONS:

1. Put all ingredients in a mug. Mix well. Microwave for a minute. You can top it with whipped cream and a sprinkle of sweetener before serving.

Nutri info per serving (1 mug cake): 447 calories, 4.77g net carbs, 42.03g fat, 12.61g protein

TRES LECHES

Yield: 12 servings
Preparation time: 45 minutes
Cooking Time: 45 minutes

INGREDIENTS:

- 1/4 teaspoon salt
- 1 1/2 teaspoons baking powder
- 1/2 cup ground golden flax or additional almond flour
- 1/2 cup coconut flour
- 1/2 cup almond flour
- 1/2 cup unsweetened almond milk
- 2 teaspoons vanilla
- 1/2 cup sweetener
- 8 whole eggs

For the topping

- 1 recipe sugar-free sweetened condensed milk
- 1/3 cup half and half

For the icing

- 2 tablespoons sweetener
- pint heavy cream

DIRECTIONS:

1. Whisk eggs, vanilla, almond milk, and 1/2 cup of sweetener in a bowl. Add salt, flours, and baking powder. Mix well. Transfer to a greased baking pan and spread out evenly. Bake in a preheated oven at 350⁰ F for 45 minutes. Leave to cool.

2. Put half and half and condensed milk in a cup. Mix until combined. Drizzle on top of the cooled cake. Leave for 30 minutes.

3. Whisk cream in a bowl until stiff. Add the sweetener and
    mix well. Spread icing on the cake. Slice and serve.

*Nutri info per serving (1/12): 275 calories, 3g net carbs, 24g fat,
7g protein*

CREAMY KETO FLAN

Yield: 6 servings
Preparation time: 20 minutes
Cooking Time: 55 minutes

INGREDIENTS:

- 1 teaspoon vanilla extract
- 1/8 teaspoon salt
- 5 eggs
- 1 cup water
- 1 3/4 cups heavy cream
- 1/4 teaspoon blackstrap molasses (optional)
- 1 cup low carb sugar substitute (divided)

DIRECTIONS:

1. Put blackstrap molasses and half a cup of granular sweetener in a pan over medium-low flame. Stir until combined and melted. Transfer to a pie pan and spread out evenly. Leave for 10 minutes.
2. Put water and cream in a pan over medium flame. Bring to a boil while stirring often.
3. Whisk eggs in a bowl. Add half a cup of granular sweetener and salt. Add the cream mixture and mix well. Transfer to the prepared pan. Place pan on a larger baking pan with an inch deep of boiling water. Bake for 55 minutes at 325 F.

Nutri info per serving (1 gram): 294 calories, 0.5g net carbs, 27.3g fat, 5.2g protein

LOW CARB MEXICAN COFFEE

Yield: 2 servings
Preparation time: 5 minutes
Cooking Time: 10 minutes

INGREDIENTS:

- 2 tablespoons sugar-free brown sugar and cinnamon syrup
- 1 tablespoon Erythritol sweetener
- 1/4 teaspoon vanilla extract
- 3 tablespoons espresso ground coffee (you can also use 1/4 cup regular coffee)
- 1 tablespoon cocoa powder (unsweetened)
- A pinch of salt
- 2 whole cloves
- 1/2 cinnamon stick
- 2 1/2 cups water

DIRECTIONS:

1. Put ground coffee, cocoa powder, salt, cloves, cinnamon, and water in a saucepan over medium-high flame. Bring to a boil. Turn heat to low. Leave to simmer for 5 minutes. Turn off the heat. Add flavored syrup, sweetener, and vanilla extract. Mix well. Leave to rest for 5 minutes.
2. Carefully transfer coffee to 2 mugs or use a coffee filter. Adjust sweetness according to taste.

Nutri info per serving (1 cup): 11 calories, 1g net carbs, 0g fat, 0g protein

SPICY MARGARITA

Yield: 1 serving
Preparation time: 5 minutes
Cooking Time: 7 minutes

INGREDIENTS:

- Ice
- 1 slice of jalapeño pepper, add more for garnishing

For the simple syrup

- 1/2 cup granulated Swerve

- 1 fl. oz. low-carb simple syrup
- 1 fl. oz. fresh lime juice
- 2 fl. oz. tequila

- 1/2 cup water

DIRECTIONS:

1. Prepare the simple syrup. Put water and Swerve in a pot over medium flame. Simmer for 7 minutes or until the mixture becomes syrupy. Leave to cool. You will only need 1/4 of the syrup. Store in the rest in a jar and refrigerate.
2. Muddle jalapeño in a cocktail shaker. Add ice, tequila, simple syrup, and lime juice. Shake well. Strain and transfer to a glass. Add ice before serving. You can garnish the drink with lime or a slice of jalapeño.

Nutri info per serving: 145 calories, 4.5g net carbs, 0g fat, 0.1g protein

CONCLUSION

I'd like to thank you and congratulate you for transiting my lines from start to finish.

I hope this book was able to help you to get excited about the ketogenic diet and in trying out the Mexican dishes featured.

The next step is to fill your pantry with the right ingredients and start planning your keto Mexican meals.

I wish you the best of luck!